HOW TO BUILD ZANE

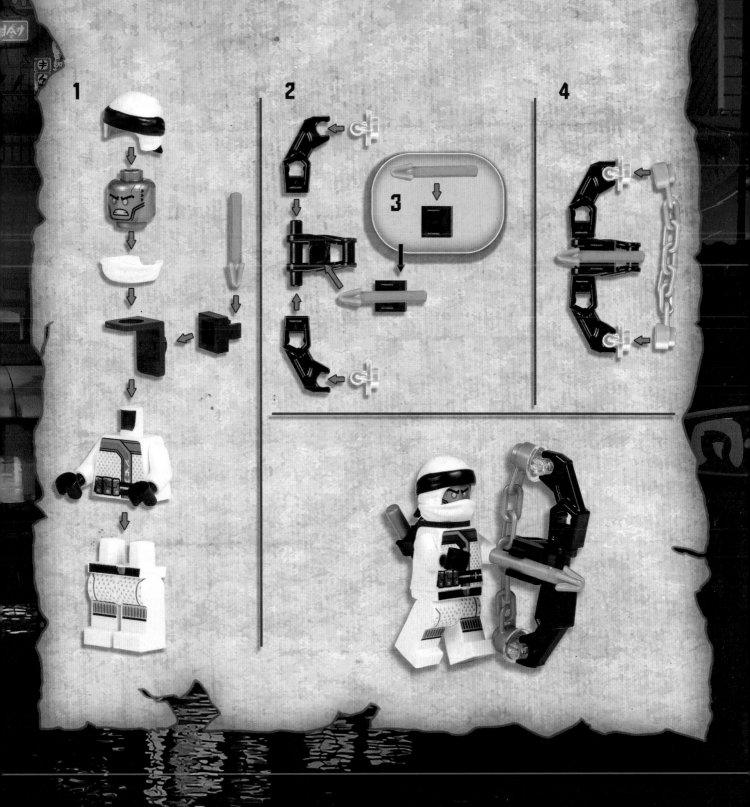

CONTENTS

MOTORCYCLE GANG

Help the ninja find out more about the Sons of Garmadon and connect matching portraits and elements between the yellow boxes placed in sequence. Remember that for each box pair there is only one pair of drawings.

Can you also spot two boxes containing the same drawings?

MYSTERIOUS MASKS

The Sons of Garmadon are looking for Oni Masks, but they don't know their exact locations. Find a path made out of symbols of one colour that will span from the first to the last row of the map grid. The symbols can connect vertically, horizontally and diagonally.

START

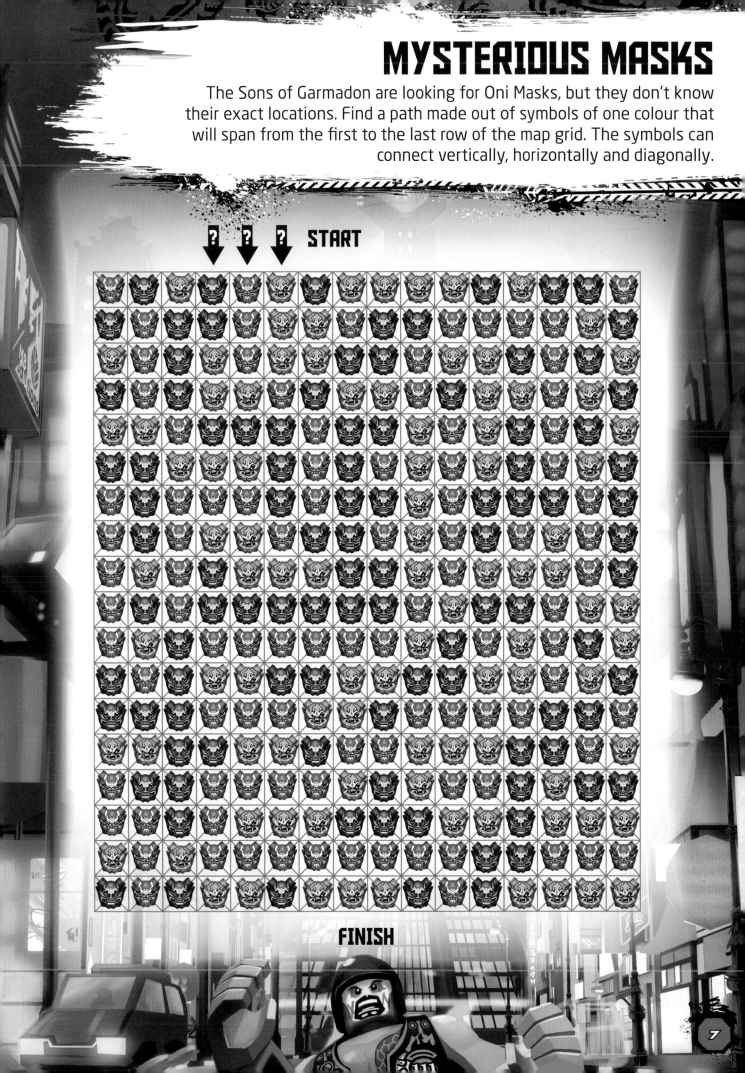

FINISH

MR. E'S CODE

Mr. E and Ultra Violet created their own special way of communicating. Can you decipher what the mysterious biker said? Decode his speech by marking the letter with the lightest background in each triangle. Write down the marked letters inside the empty spaces.

POSING AS THE ENEMY

Zane wants to infiltrate the ranks of the Sons of Garmadon. Help him gather information about the gang members. Write the correct numbers of the domino pieces with villain portraits inside the empty spaces.

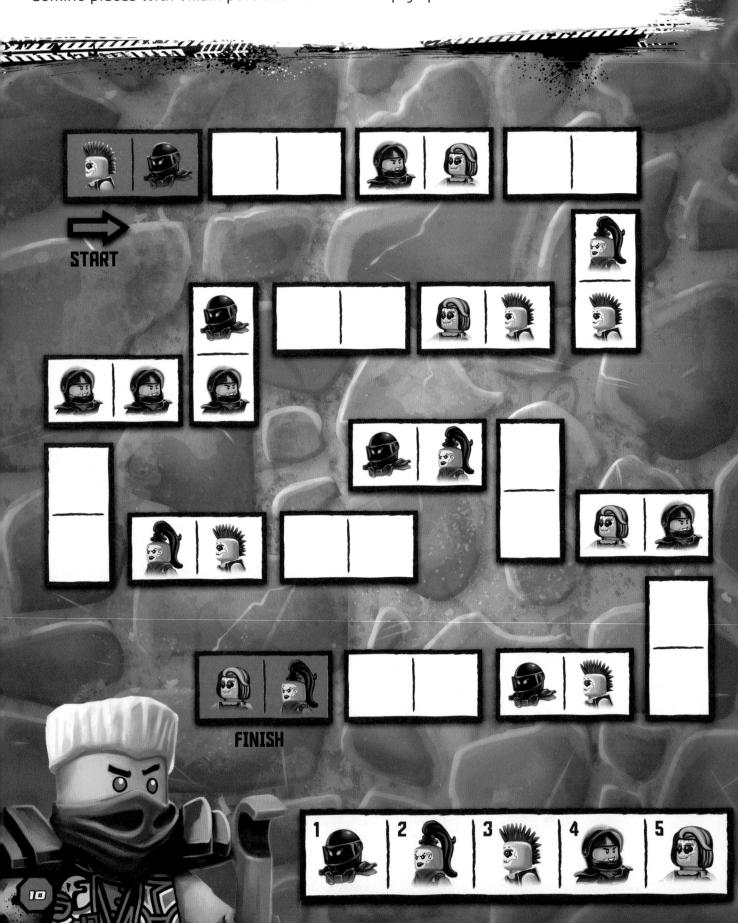

START

FINISH

10

SYSTEM RESTORE

Zane's cover was blown and he ended up badly damaged in the fight against Mr. E. Help the other ninja save him and enter a special code into his operating system. Remember that the code needed is a multiple of the pattern below.

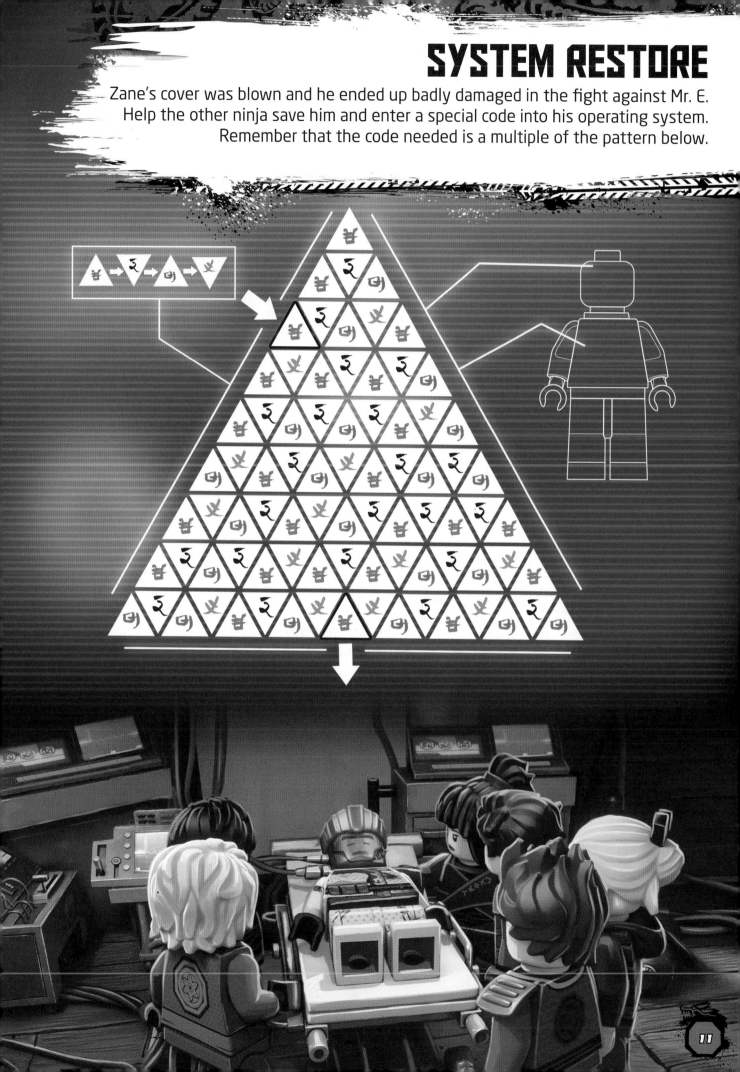

SAMURAI'S SECRET

Samurai X is always out to assist the ninja team in their fight against the Sons of Garmadon. Take a good look at the two pictures of the amazing fight scene and find 10 differences between them.

Do you know who the mysterious Samurai X really is? One detail in the illustration will help you discover the answer.
Add a tick next to the right portrait.

13

A TOUGH LANDING

Destiny's Bounty crash-landed in the jungle! Help the ninja get out from beneath the broken bamboo. Mark the order in which the stalks of bamboo should be discarded, starting with the one on top of the stack. Write the numbers inside the white shapes.

ON THE WAY TO THE TEMPLE

Lloyd and Harumi can't find the way to the Oni Temple. Help them by drawing a line on the map using clues from the frame. Remember: there is only one path to take.

START

FINISH

TRUE COLOURS

The Green Ninja discovered that Harumi is the leader of the Sons of Garmadon. He must stop the princess from resurrecting evil Lord Garmadon. Count how many times Harumi and Lloyd's names appear in the chart, and write the numbers in the boxes. Whoever's name appears the most will win the duel!

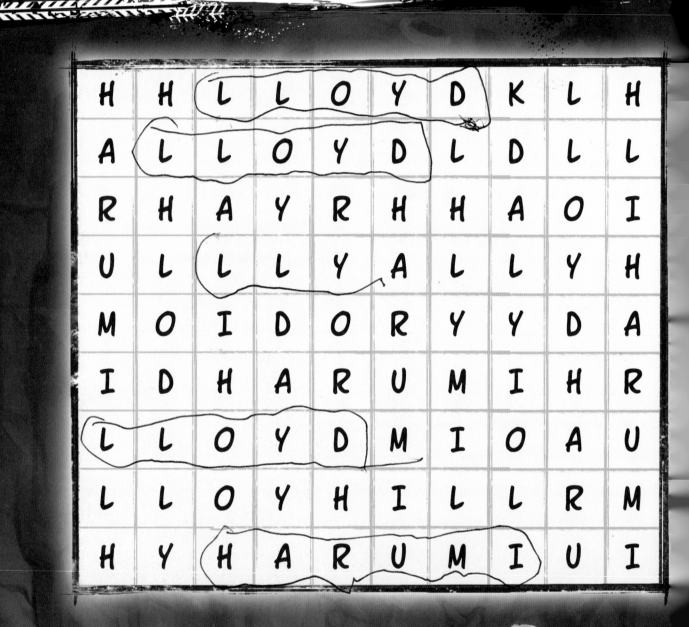

H	H	L	L	O	Y	D	K	L	H
A	L	L	O	Y	D	L	D	L	L
R	H	A	Y	R	H	H	A	O	I
U	L	L	L	Y	A	L	L	Y	H
M	O	I	D	O	R	Y	Y	D	A
I	D	H	A	R	U	M	I	H	R
L	L	O	Y	D	M	I	O	A	U
L	L	O	Y	H	I	L	L	R	M
H	Y	H	A	R	U	M	I	U	I

HARUMI

LLOYD

KEY TO FREEDOM

The ninja were ambushed by the Sons of Garmadon, who tied them up in chains. Little Wu is now their only hope! Help the kid open the lock by marking the key that is the same shape as the keyhole (but remember that it's a mirror image!).

JUNGLE SURPRISE

The ninja need to keep their eyes peeled during their jungle crossing.
They're quite surprised to notice some unexpected objects on the way.
Mark 7 things that do not fit the scene.

An overgrown crab can be an excellent means of transport, especially if you offer it a treat on a fishing rod. Untangle the lines to find out how the ninja managed to tame the beast using this giant crustacean's favourite delicacy. Yum!

THROWING DICE

Misako, who is now taking care of Little Wu, is trying to keep the boy entertained. She wants to play dice with him. Have a close look at the picture below and mark the die Wu is thinking about.

THE YOUNG ARTIST

Misako gave crayons to Little Wu and asked him to draw his favourite ninja mech. Can you tell which machine he likes the most? To find out, help him draw its outline.

POLICE BACKUP

The Ninjago City Police Commissioner is leading a group of policemen in a last-ditch attempt against the Sons of Garmadon. Help him find the characters from the box below in the scene.

HURRY UP! WE NEED TO STOP HARUMI AND HER GANG BEFORE SHE STARTS A RITUAL TO RESURRECT THE EVIL LORD GARMADON.

SPEEDY SUBMERSIBLE

In order to reach the Temple of Resurrection unnoticed, Kai needs to steer his *Katana V11* along the old Ninjago City canals. Quick! Navigate him through this water maze.

FINISH

START

GARMADON'S RESURRECTION

With the powers of the Oni Masks combined, the resurrection ritual can begin. Help the ninja point out the masks on the circle that don't match the others.

After defeating Harumi and the Sons of Garmadon, the ninja took a group photo, but it fell and shattered. Fix the memento by marking the missing fragments with the right letters for where they should be. Watch out! There are 5 false pieces, too!

THE GREAT ESCAPE

Harumi opened the Kryptarium Prison cells to set the Sons of Garmadon free. Look at the diagram below and complete it by working out the sequence and writing the correct letters of the padlocks in the empty spaces to learn the code that she used.

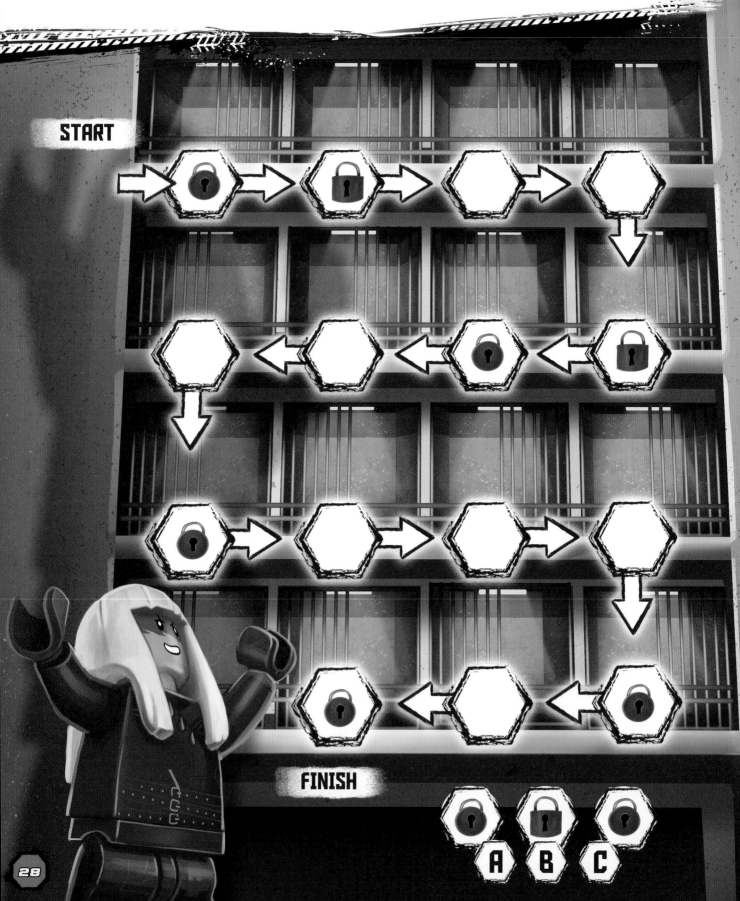

START

FINISH

A B C

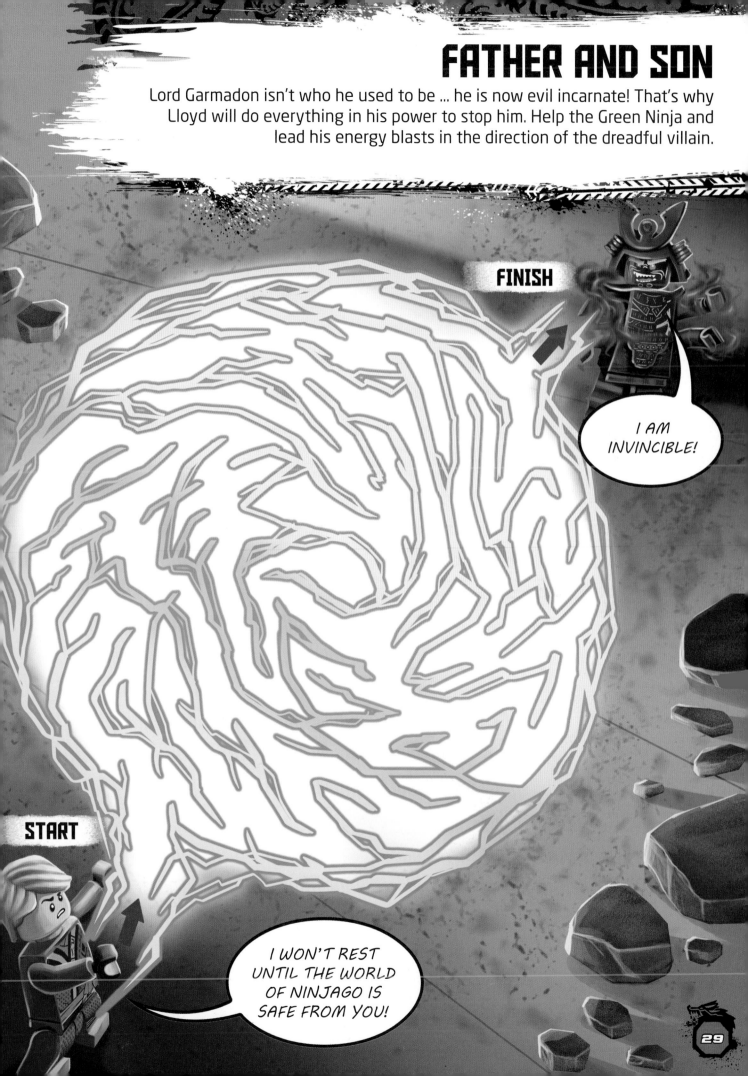

THE DARK CONQUEROR

Evil Lord Garmadon wants to rule Ninjago Island! Connect the dots to see the villain towering over the town.

LET THE WORLD OF NINJAGO SEE THEIR NEW MASTER!

MAGIC POTION

During his duel with Garmadon, Lloyd was badly hurt. The rest of the ninja went to Mystake's Tea Shop to ask for her help. Find and mark the four sets of different teapots containing the healing potion, shown in the boxes below on the grid.

THE MAGIC TEA WILL GET LLOYD UP ON HIS FEET AGAIN!

THE ONI TITAN

The indestructible Oni Titan is built out of elements Lord Garmadon placed in a very particular way. Put the letters of the stone giant's parts inside the grid so that they don't repeat in any column, row or 2x3 rectangle outlined in bold.

THE COLOSSUS OF DESTRUCTION

Try to stop the Oni Titan from destroying Ninjago City by tangling it with power lines. Connect the identical-coloured transmission towers so that the cables don't cross.

INTO THE UNKNOWN

Traveller's Tea is the only way the ninja can escape the Oni Titan. After they opened the pouch of tea, everyone was surrounded by a flurry of the magical plant's spinning blossom. Find 10 six-petalled flowers among them.

A STRANGE LAND

After being damaged by the fearsome Oni Titan, *Destiny's Bounty* barely managed to land in the Realm of Oni and Dragon. It's missing many parts that need to be gathered. Count how many of each part shown inside the box are in the picture. Write their numbers in the shapes.

KNOW YOUR ENEMY

The ninja escaped Lord Garmadon by arriving in a strange realm. Little do they know that even here, new enemies await them. Match the portraits with their descriptions so that the Spinjitzu Masters know more about their new opponents.

A THE RUTHLESS LEADER OF THE DRAGON HUNTERS. HE HAS AN IRON PEG LEG AND WEARS A TOP HAT.

B IRON BARON'S RIGHT HAND. WEARS A BROAD HAT AND A METAL MASK THAT COVERS THE LOWER PART OF HIS FACE.

C A WARRIOR WALKING ON FOUR MECHANICAL LEGS, WHICH HE EXPERTLY USES IN COMBAT.

D SMILING DRAGON HUNTER WEARING A HORNED HELMET WITH ONE HORN MISSING. HE'S A BIT ON THE CRAZY SIDE.

E A TOUGH WARRIOR WITH A MOHAWK, A JETPACK AND AN ATTITUDE. SHE DREAMS OF BECOMING THE LEADER OF THE DRAGON HUNTER CLAN.

F THIS WELDING HELMET-WEARING WARRIOR BASES HIS EVERY DECISION ON PURE CHANCE, USING THE SLOT MACHINE ON HIS CHEST PLATE TO GUIDE HIS ACTIONS.

G HE'S VERY TALKATIVE, BUT ONLY THE OTHER DRAGON HUNTERS KNOW WHAT HE'S SAYING. HIS MASK IS SIMILAR TO HEAVY METAL'S BUT HE DOESN'T WEAR A HAT.

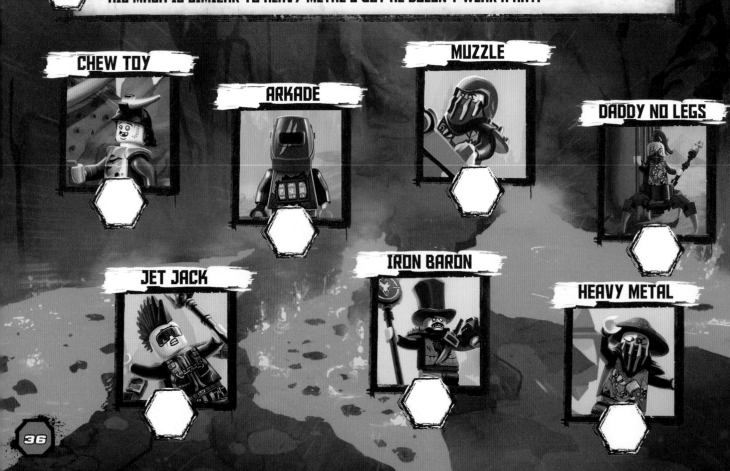

CHEW TOY

ARKADE

MUZZLE

DADDY NO LEGS

JET JACK

IRON BARON

HEAVY METAL

LITTLE MASTER IS TRAINING!

Wu is growing up really fast! He has just begun his martial arts training with Cole as his teacher. Help him perform the right sequence of moves by writing down the numbers for the right stances.

WHO'S THE GREEN NINJA?

BY SUE BEHRENT

"Who's hungry?" asked Dareth, looking around the dirty garage.

Nya's hand shot up from behind the motorcycle she was working on.

Across the table, Lloyd looked up and shrugged.

"Right, so that's one crispy noodle, two pork buns, bubble tea for Nya, and fried tofu and jasmine tea for Lloyd," said Dareth. "And five shallot pancakes for me."

"I'll come with you," said Lloyd, getting up from the table. "I need some air. This place isn't exactly five-star accommodation."

"We're hiding from Princess Harumi and the Sons of Garmadon in a slum, Lloyd, I don't think it's exactly on a level with the best hotels in Ninjago City," Dareth replied.

"We've talked about this, Lloyd," said Nya, standing up and wiping her hands on her overalls. "You have to stay hidden. If Harumi finds you and takes you to your father, Emperor Garmadon, he'll destroy you and everybody you love."

Lloyd sat down heavily and sighed.

"It's just … I just feel so useless sitting around waiting for something to happen."

"Everything happens at its destined time and not before," said Nya.

"Did you get that from Master Wu?" asked Lloyd, grinning.

"Nope. A fortune cookie," said Nya with a smile.

***

From the shadows, Dareth peered into a large courtyard overlooked on four sides by high-rise flats.

"No menacing bikers or evil ex-princesses," he muttered to himself as walked over to his regular food cart. "Only the sweet smell of pork buns and shallot pancakes."

"HEY YOU!" someone yelled.

"Show no fear," Dareth said to himself as he caught sight of two Sons of Garmadon entering the courtyard from another entrance.

"We patrol this slum every day," said one of the gang as they approached Dareth. "And we haven't seen you around here before."

"That's strange, because I'm a regular at this food cart," said Dareth.

"We'd better take him to Harumi and see what she wants done with him," said the second gang member.

"But ... um ... I'm the Green Ninja," Dareth blurted nervously ... and immediately regretted it.

The Sons of Garmadon exchanged doubtful looks.

"Yeah, I don't think so," said the first one.

"I've beaten ten Sons of Garmadon at once with the force of my Spinjitzu," said Dareth, getting into the part. "Do you two seriously think you'll be able to take me to Harumi?"

The first gang member took a small step back.

"OK, OK, be cool," he said, sizing up the situation.

"I'll be crazy if I want to!" shouted Dareth. "Nobody tells the Green Ninja what to do."

"I think he might be the Green Ninja," said the second gang member. "He takes after his dad. The Emperor hates being told what to do as well."

"But would the Green Ninja say he was the Green Ninja?" asked the first.

"Yes, he would," Dareth cut in. "I mean, yes I would."

"I can't decide," said the second Son. "Let's take him to Harumi anyway."

The Sons of Garmadon grabbed Dareth and started to drag him off.

"Let me go!" Dareth shrieked, struggling to free himself.

All of sudden, a rope dropped from the window of a flat and Lloyd abseiled into the courtyard.

"Let him go!" he yelled. "I'm the Green Ninja!"

The two gang members looked at Dareth and then at Lloyd.

"He's the Green Ninja," they both said as they threw Dareth to the ground and rushed at Lloyd.

"I'm the Green Ninja!" yelled the woman at the food cart.

"No, I'm the Green Ninja!" cried a young man waiting for his lunch order.

"I'm the Green Ninja!" shouted a man walking by.

Soon the cry of "I'm the Green Ninja" could be heard from every window and doorway facing into the courtyard.

"Is there an echo in here?" the first gang member asked in confusion.

"This is freaking me out! Let's get out of here!" said the second.

The Sons of Garmadon released Lloyd and ran out of the courtyard.

"The resistance never quits!" Lloyd called at their retreating backs.

"Yeah, the resistance never quits!" chimed in Dareth.

"The resistance never quits, the resistance never quits!" the people chanted.

"The resistance might not quit," said the second gang member once they were clear of the courtyard. "But I've had enough, man. Tell the Emperor I quit!"

BIRTH OF THE RESISTANCE

Find and mark the names of characters that will form a resistance movement against the evil Garmadon. Their portraits are shown below. The letters of their names appear horizontally and vertically but not diagonally.

PIXAL

LLOYD

MYSTAKE

NYA

DARETH

L	O	Y	P	D	A	L	Y	N	M	I
P	I	X	E	T	D	I	S	M	L	L
D	A	R	E	T	H	A	L	Y	B	E
A	L	O	X	I	N	M	O	S	T	I
R	L	L	O	Y	D	Y	O	T	A	K
E	O	Y	M	I	S	S	Y	A	Y	O
S	Y	M	T	T	O	T	T	K	L	L
A	Y	N	Y	E	T	A	X	E	M	I
H	S	Y	L	L	O	Y	P	I	X	E
A	R	A	N	P	I	X	A	L	L	I
L	M	T	M	I	T	E	X	I	L	N

TRAPPED BEAST

Oh no! Ruthless hunters have captured an Earth Dragon. Can you help the beast? Mark the parts of the scene that are shown on the smaller pictures. Take a good look – two of the pictures contain small differences.

FEARSOME ALLIES

Perhaps the ninja can find new friends in the Realm of Oni and Dragon as well... but they'll have to tame them first! One of them is Stormbringer, the lightning dragon. To see him in his full glory, use the numbers to colour in the picture.

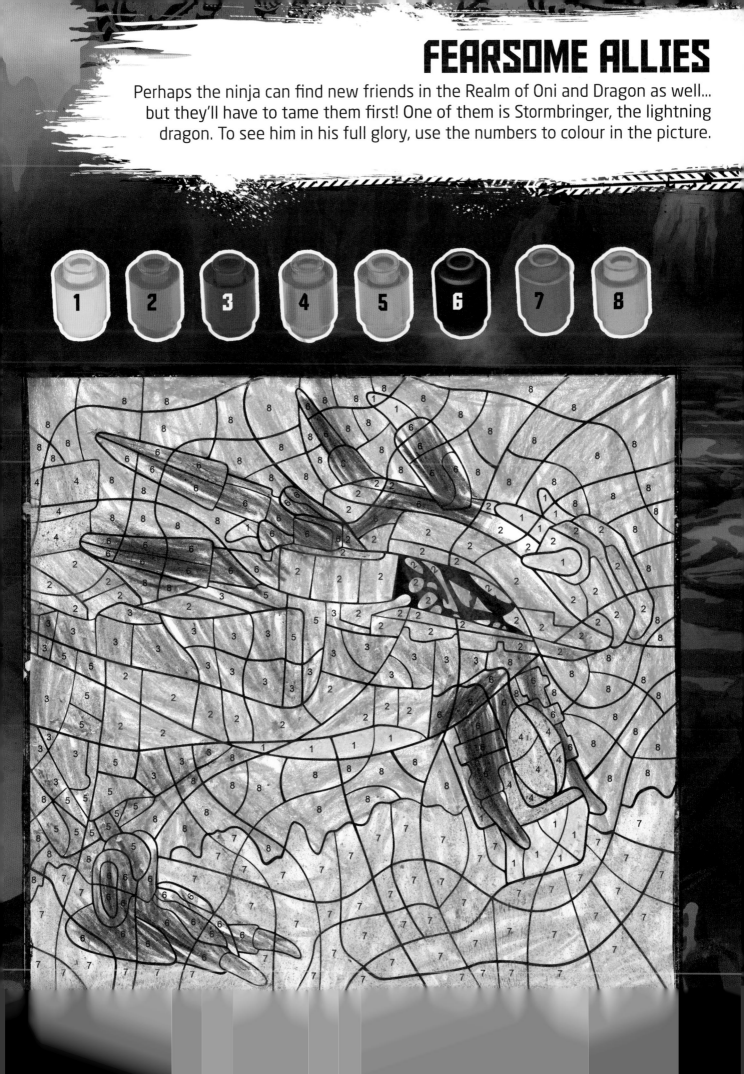

WHO'S TO BLAME?

The Sons of Garmadon, once again, failed to capture Lloyd. The evil emperor isn't pleased. Do you want to find out who will be blamed for this defeat? Look for clues inside the speech bubble to find and mark the villain who will receive punishment.

DRAGON MOTHER

Time for you to meet Firstbourne - the mother of all dragons. Take a look at all the shadows cast by her and mark the real one. Two of the fake shadows are identical. Can you tell which ones?

AN ANCIENT ARMOUR

The Dragon Armour will grant one rule over the Realm of Oni and Dragon.
Help Cole stop the villains by connecting the dots to uncover the symbol
that appears on the Dragon Armour shield.

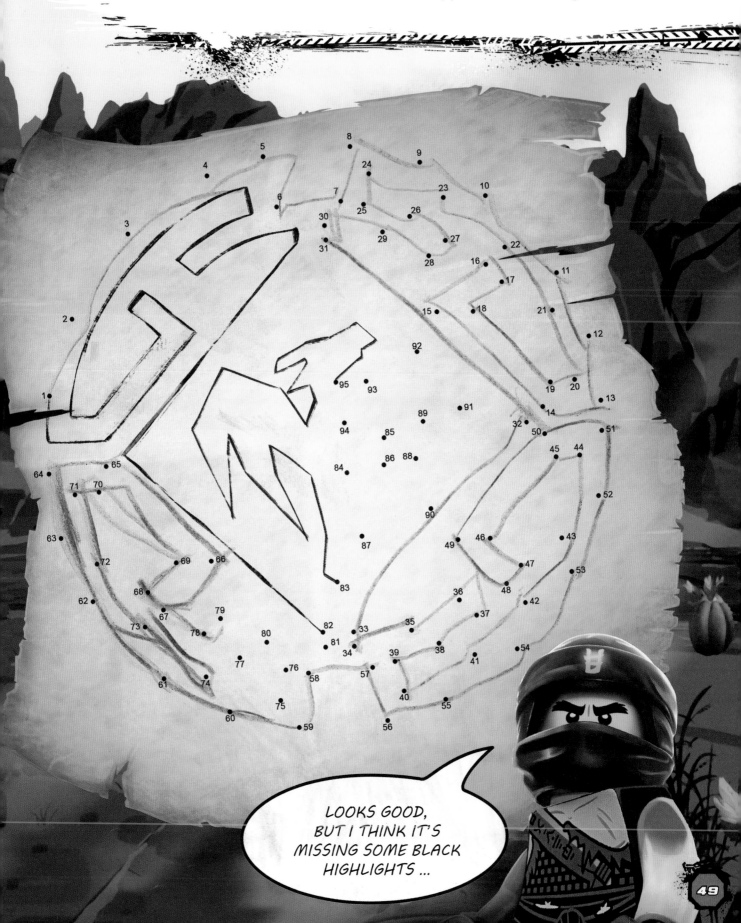

LOOKS GOOD,
BUT I THINK IT'S
MISSING SOME BLACK
HIGHLIGHTS ...

ESCAPE ATTEMPT

The ninja are still in captivity but one of them managed to escape the Dragon Pit. And what a narrow escape that was! Mark the chain closest to capturing Kai inside *Destiny's Wing*.

NOOO! OUR BRAND NEW SHIP! DON'T LET IT GET AWAY!

Ten ninja weapons have been taken away by the Dragon Hunters and hidden. Find and mark them all!

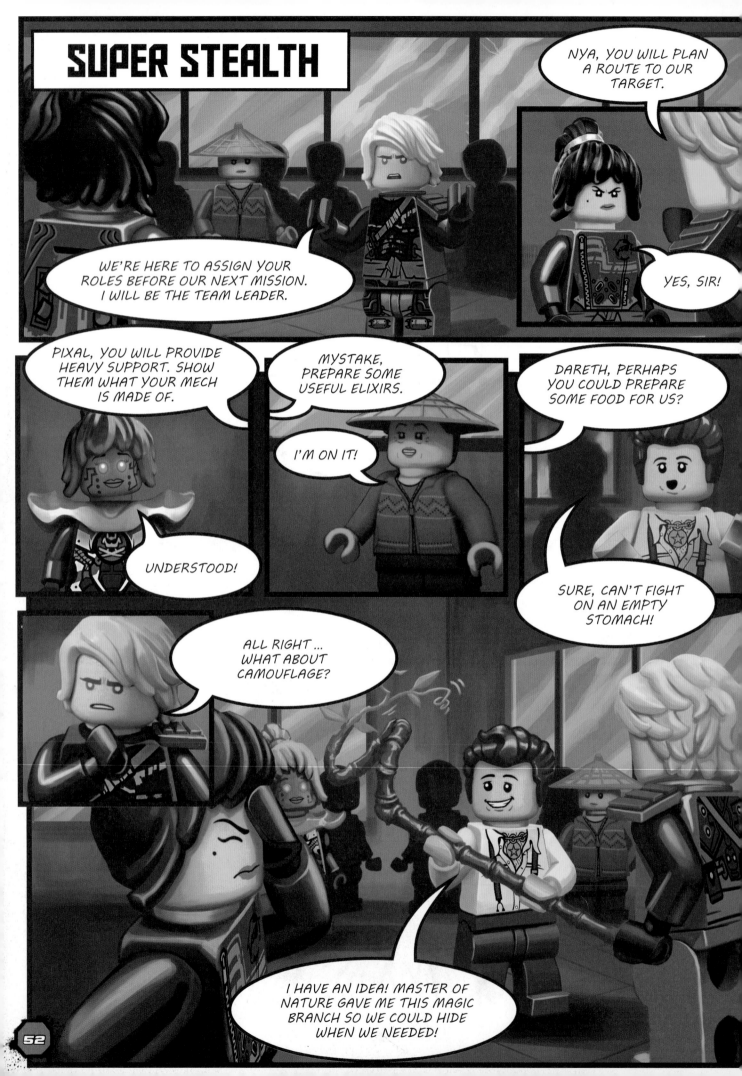

53

THE DIESELNAUT

The relentless Dragon Hunters went after the ninja in their terrifying war rig – the Dieselnaut. It's heavily armed and has eighteen wheels! Take a look at it and its reflection and mark 10 differences between them.

ENGINE MAINTENANCE

The Dieselnaut is quite a unique vehicle. It's built out of numerous mismatched parts and requires a ... particular touch. Help the Dragon Hunters oil its engine by guiding the oil stream between cogwheels from the start to the finish.

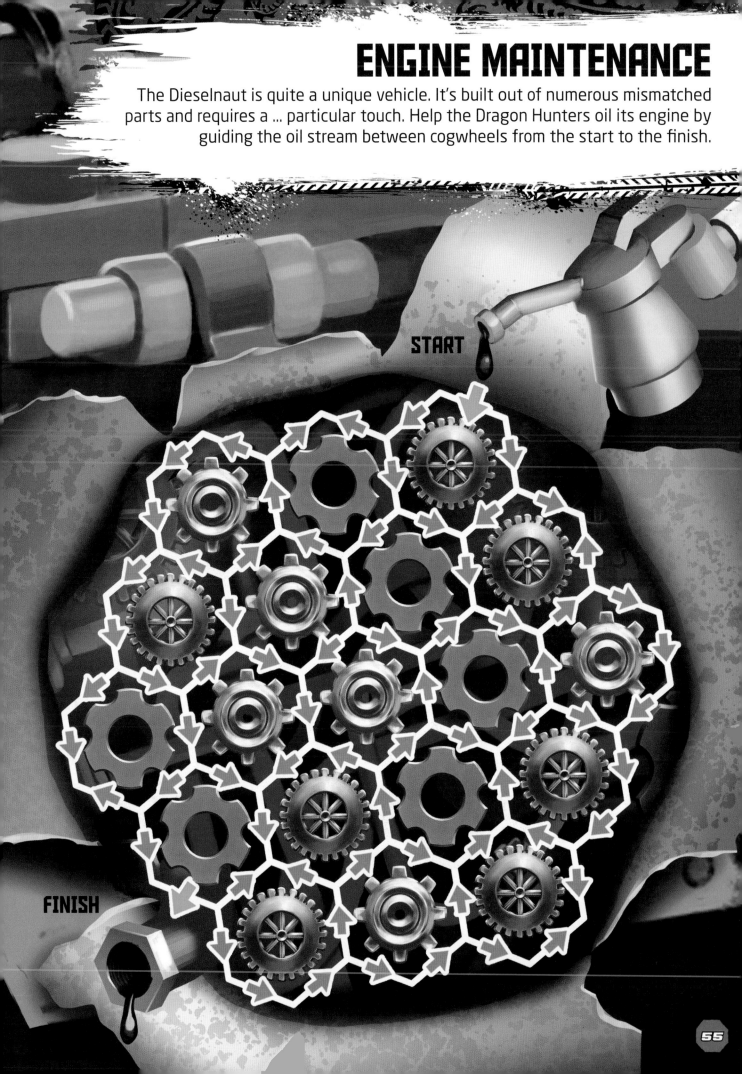

START

FINISH

STRAIGHT TO THE TOP

The Resistance members want to break into the TV studio and inform the citizens of Ninjago City about their fight against Garmadon. Show them the way to the top of the tyrant's HQ. Only use the emergency stairwells so they won't be seen.

WE'RE STILL WAITING FOR PIXAL. CAN YOU SPOT HER SOMEWHERE AROUND HERE?

FINISH

START

ANSWERS

P. 6

P. 7

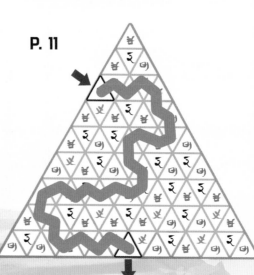

P. 8

K A R A O K E
1 2 3 4 5 6 7

P. 12-13

P. 10

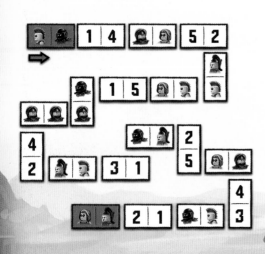

P. 11

P. 14-15

P. 16

H	H	L	L	O	Y	D	K	L	H
A	L	L	O	Y	D	L	D	L	L
R	H	A	Y	R	H	H	A	O	I
U	L	L	L	Y	A	L	L	Y	H
M	O	I	D	O	R	Y	Y	D	A
I	D	H	A	R	U	M	I	H	R
L	L	O	Y	D	M	I	O	A	U
L	L	O	Y	H	I	L	L	R	M
H	Y	H	A	R	U	M	I	U	I

HARUMI   LLOYD

5   **4**

58

ANSWERS

P. 17

P. 18

P. 19

P. 22

P. 24

P. 25

P. 26

P. 27

ANSWERS

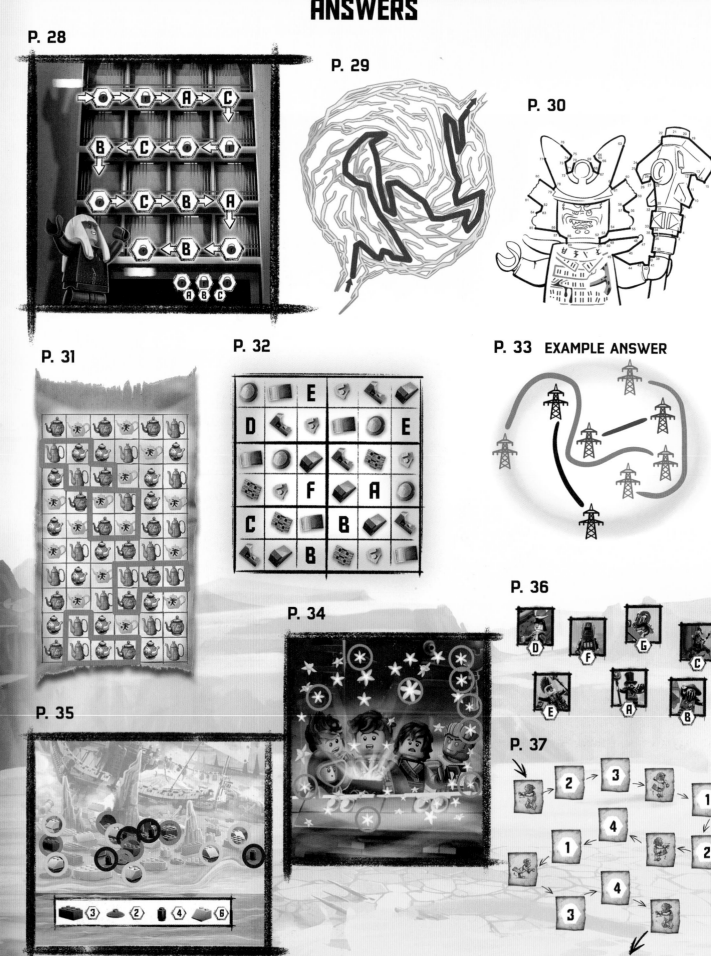

P. 28

P. 29

P. 30

P. 31

P. 32

P. 33 EXAMPLE ANSWER

P. 34

P. 35

P. 36

P. 37

ANSWERS

P. 43

P. 44

P. 45

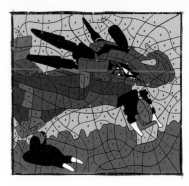

P. 46

MR. E

P. 48

P. 49

P. 50–51

P. 54

P. 55

P. 56–57